IRISH COTTAGES

IRISH COTTAGES

Photography
Liam Blake

Introduction by
John A. Jackson

REAL IRELAND

First Published by
Real Ireland Design Limited
1 Duncairn Place, Bray, Co. Wicklow, Ireland.
1985

© Photography Liam Blake Photography Ltd. 1985
© Text Prof. John A. Jackson 1985
Preface Joe Reynolds 1985

Design Joe Reynolds, introduction Prof. John A. Jackson, Photography Liam Blake.
Colour Separations Colour Repro (Dublin).

Period prints from the 'Lawrence Collection' courtesy The Gallery of Photography,
Dublin, also the National Library of Ireland.

ISBN 0-946887 03 9

Preface

If ever there was an all embracing story to be told about the people of Ireland over the last few hundred years, surely the Irish Cottage would play a significant role in that story.

The Irish Cottage protected our ancestors from the elements, and on occasions hostile landlords, although we can see from some of the period pictures at the beginning of this book, that these landlords were a lot stronger than the cottages. The cottage has stayed with us throughout these times and in some cases as we can see from the colour section of this book, changed very little.

It's so easy to take these cottages dotted around our landscape, in harmony with the mountains and valleys, for granted, so much so that if any Irish child were asked to paint a country scene, the chances are that a cottage would sooner or later appear in that picture.

An Irish cottage is made from the land, built by the people, for the people, and because of these reasons, its existance could never clash with the landscape. Not so the case for some of the modern buildings we see around our countryside today. I hope that, what the reader will become aware of, when he or she looks through this book is a story about Ireland, told almost without words.

Joe Reynolds.

IRISH COTTAGES

John A. Jackson
Department of Sociology,
Trinity College Dublin.

The idea of the cottage is popularly enshrined in the romanti-cised picture of the English rural village with thatched roofs, old timbers, hollyhocks and roses in abundance in the cottage garden. The Irish cottage lacks the same tradition of relatively settled and supported rural society located in villages as part of a manorial holding. The situation in Ireland is typified more by an isolated and distributed settlement on the land, a less developed craft and architectural tradition and a harsher and less receptive countryside and climate.

The dynamic relationship between land and people is essential to understanding the patterns and types of habitation that have been developed in different places. Not only will one particular form be found only in certain parts of the country

IRISH COTTAGES

John A. Jackson
Department of Sociology,
Trinity College Dublin.

The idea of the cottage is popularly enshrined in the romanticised picture of the English rural village with thatched roofs, old timbers, hollyhocks and roses in abundance in the cottage garden. The Irish cottage lacks the same tradition of relatively settled and supported rural society located in villages as part of a manorial holding. The situation in Ireland is typified more by an isolated and distributed settlement on the land, a less developed craft and architectural tradition and a harsher and less receptive countryside and climate.

The dynamic relationship between land and people is essential to understanding the patterns and types of habitation that have been developed in different places. Not only will one particular form be found only in certain parts of the country

but different historical experiences will be reflected in the retention of one form in some districts long after its disappearance elsewhere. The contemporary landscape is made up of residues of a long and complex past history which is echoed in the buildings and the land and in the relationship between them.

Although the predominant residential pattern in the Irish countryside is now one of dispersed settlement with single farmhouses and cottages sitting in the midst of a holding of land, this has not always been the case. The older pattern which owes its origins to ancient tribal society and to the rundale agrarian system is the 'clachan' – a cluster of cottages, higgledy-piggledy, huddled together as if for protection.

Unlike the English village with its Church, Manor and pub on the green the clachan is a residential grouping of some ten to twenty houses originally occupied by members of the same extended family.

Such clachans were widely distributed in the north and west of the country before the Famine and elsewhere were found in those areas that resisted enclosure of the common land involved in an openfield system of agriculture. Efforts by landlords to reform the rundale system, especially after it had led to constant sub-division of the land, with increasing population, were seldom completely successful and examples can still be found of the clachan and the sub-divided field systems associated with it.

Contemporary accounts attest to the poverty and wretchedness that characterised the cottiers life in pre-Famine Ireland. It is therefore hardly surprising that the peasant's cottage was a small and basic dwelling built for the necessities of an existence that was both uncertain and impermanent. Evictions, emigration and atrocity all combined to make tenuous the relationship of a tenant family to the land and cottage they occupied. Daniel Corkery has described it well:

> *'The peasant had to wring from the soil the gold that supported this huge and artificial superstructure – the bailiff in the village, the steward in the town, the agent in Dublin, the Lord in England. Living from hand to mouth with no reserves the cottier was at the mercy not only of winds and rains but of every change and even threat of change in the body politic, the body economic.'*
>
> (Daniel Corkery, *Hidden Ireland*, Gill and Macmillan, 1979, p. 38)

Poverty and the paucity of materials available for construction determined that most Irish cottiers lived in dwellings built from easily available articles – timber, rough stones, twigs, rushes and furze, sods and thatch for the roof and mud for the floor. Few before the middle of the last century would have had chimneys or glazed windows.

Little of these pre-Famine dwellings remains but their character is etched on the countryside and the cottages that followed them have kept much of their sparse economy in design. A distinction can be made between two main types in the traditional Irish cottage. The first, found characteristically in the north-west of the country, along the west coast and on the south-western peninsulas, has a chimney in the

end gable with a long room that occasionally has a small piece built out by the fireplace to take a bed. This long room was a development of the byre cottage found throughout northern Europe and shared with farm animals. As late as 1938 Estyn Evans describes an old bachelor living in such a cottage in Donegal with himself at one end near the hearth and his donkey and cow at the other. The second type, found throughout the midlands and the eastern seaboard, is characterised by a central chimney and hip roof arch. This latter construction with the central division created by the fireplace breaks naturally into two rooms and the higher roof structure permitted an upper floor to be developed with a stairwell rising out of the living room. Inside the cottage of either type the hearth formed a centre with a crane

supporting pots and kettle, a griddle to lay over the fire for bread and a hand-turned blower to keep the fire glowing.

Variety in style and form within these limits is evident in different parts of the country. There is generally little that is ornate. Distinctiveness is to be seen more in windows and doorways and gates, rather than in the building itself. The walls are generally thick and solid and the windows small – to keep the weather out rather than to let the light in; to see out on a 'valley of squinting windows' rather than to provide the windows of display typical of The Netherlands. Doors and half-doors necessary for light gave the opportunity for expression, strong colour and decoration, an individuality of form that put a mark on the place. Later, particularly when

grants were available, gate posts of enormous substance might be added to adorn the approach to quite humble habitations.

With better timber and more solid building materials the basic form was elaborated into a farmhouse with two storeys, two up and two down; into a shop, or into the urban cottage found in Georgian artisan dwellings in Dublin which characteristically added a basement to give more rooms. The narrow dimensions of the cottage retain much the same character with the central door and two living rooms opening off it.

The contemporary Irish landscape bears witness to the basic

features of the cottage form but always allows enormous scope for variation. Each generation and each locality makes its impact on the buildings and their relationship to the land. Change of use, emigration, and new building all play a part. Tourism and the economic boom for agriculture following the initial years in the European Economic Community have transformed much of the countryside. Old cottages have been rebuilt or replaced by returned emigrants or foreign settlers. Picture windows have been incorporated to view the landscape on the Atlantic coast facing out on the prevailing winds that the old cottages often had their backs turned to for greater warmth. Central heating, paint and colour, electricity and running water have changed the cottage to a place of comfort rather than necessity. In a number of farms the old dwelling has been left, or turned into a store, and the family have moved into a new suburban bungalow set incongruously in a field on the farm, responding to the new images of city life, the media and the comforts of the consumer society.

Much recent new building in the countryside appears to follow a formula reflecting the package holiday to Spain with 'haciendas' with a series of Moorish arches of gleaming whiteness that suggest a sunglazed climate far removed from the reality of the wet and wind of an Irish winter. In the part of the country I know best a fine farm with drive leading up to it is known locally as 'South Fork' after the television series 'Dallas'. Increasingly international influences and diverse cultural inputs obliterate the ancient tradition of the

Irish cottage preserved by local builders little affected by architectural fashions.

But something of the spirit remains. A blend of sociability and independence. The sociability found in the close relationship of the clachan is replicated today in the country pub and is as described in Gweedore in pre-Famine Donegal:

'They are great talkers; as firing is plentiful, they sit up half the night in winter, talking and telling stories, they therefore dislike living in detached houses. They are however, a quiet inoffensive race when not interfered with, naturally civil and kind in their manner.'

(Fr. James McAdam cited by E. Estyn Evans, *The Personality of Ireland*, Cambridge University Press, 1973, p. 96)

Independence is shown in the brightly coloured individuality by which the Irish cottage can be observed across a valley or under a mountain in the brilliant Irish light that follows rain. It is a practical, realistic accommodation to the natural world. A statement that does not demand too much of the environment but quietly asserts a presence of continuity and endurance against the elements of weather, economy and time. Neither romanticised, nor embellished, the Irish cottage stands witness to the rich variety of human culture that it contains within its walls – a hidden Ireland that protects the pride of a tradition driven underground during the Penal Times, oppressed by Anglicisation but strong in the people themselves and the verbal traditions of language, conversation and song that depended not so much on material possession

as the indomitability of the human spirit. Again Corkery describing the range of subject that was likely to be found discussed in the meanest dwelling remarks *'They were not hedonists, they were men worn by wind and earth and sea, not so defeated in brain however that they could no longer enjoy the free working of the mind'. (ibid. p. 235)*

Thatched cottage, Bloody Foreland, Co. Donegal.

Tin roof of an old cottage, Bolus Head, Co. Kerry. The island in the distance is Scariff.

Cottage, Glencolumbkille, Co. Donegal.

A small cottage of the simplest type, Ballyconneely Bay, Co. Galway.

Cottage in Doolin with the Liscannor-slate roof commonly used in West Clare.

Thatched cottage in the village of Craughwell, Co. Galway.

Two-storey cottage on the Ring of Kerry. In the background are the Skelligs and Puffin Island.

Thatched cottage at Ballyness Bay, Co. Donegal.

Thatched cottage in Carna, Co. Galway.

Thatched cottage in Kinvara, Co. Galway.

A pretty cottage window on Aran Islands.

Cottage window, Ballydavid, Dingle peninsula, Co. Kerry.

Thatched cottage in the Glenesh valley, Co. Donegal.

Thatched cottage on Clare Island Co. Mayo.

Tin roofed cottage near Trim, Co. Meath.

Tin roofed cottage, Glen of Imal, Co. Wicklow.

Outbuildings, near Dunloe, Co. Donegal.

Outbuildings, Bloody Foreland, Co. Donegal.

An interior view of a cottage window at Bunratty Folk Park, Co. Clare, indicates the thickness of old cottage walls.

Outbuildings, North Donegal.

Changing tastes. A new bungalow stands beside a traditional cottage near Portmarnock, Co. Dublin.

…and compromises. A caravan is sited within the walls of this half demolished cottage in north Donegal.

Homecoming, Inishbofin Island, Co. Mayo.

Cottage on Clare Island, Co. Mayo.

The harsh climatic conditions which some cottages must face is clearly shown in this study of a two-storey cottage and wind bent trees near Glencolombkille, Co. Donegal.

Two storey cottage near Allihies, Co. Cork.

A farmer stands outside of his cottage near Dursey Island, Co. Cork.

Geese outside of a cottage in north Donegal.

Cottage door, Allihies, West Cork.

Ship's porthole set into door of cottage near Crohy Head, Co. Donegal.

Thatched cottage of hipped roofed type, common over most of east and central Ireland, Listowel, Co. Kerry.

Gate Lodge of estate near Wicklow town.

Sea mists creep towards a cottage on the Beara Peninsula, Co. Cork.

Cottages at Malin Head, Co. Donegal.

The cottage in ruins. Derelicts in Co. Meath and Co. Donegal.

Flowers enhance a cottage window in Kilmore Quay, Co. Wexford.

An austere little cottage window in Spiddal, Co. Galway.

Cottage, Ballyvaughan, Co. Clare.

Cottage in the Slieve Bloom Mountains, Co. Laois.

The cottage and the landscape. Winter and summer views of the same cottage at Sally Gap, Co. Wicklow.

Unusual detail from a thatched cottage in the 'estate' village of Adare, Co. Limerick.

An exquisitely painted cottage near Mallow, Co. Cork.

'Infield' farming at a cottage near Lettermullan, Co. Galway. In the foreground are 'Lazy Beds', an ancient method of cultivation which has been used in Ireland since Bronze age times.

Thatched cottages at Ballyconneely Bay, Co. Galway.

Thatched cottage near Crohy Head, Co. Donegal.

This unwhitewashed cottage at Roundstone, Co. Galway shows the primitive but sturdy stonework typical of the cottage in the West of Ireland.

Cottage near Kilmore Quay, Co. Wexford.

Thatched cottage, Kilcolgan, Co. Galway.

Cottage, Bloody Foreland, Co. Donegal.

Cottage near Arthurstown, Co. Wexford.

An attractive cottage near Waterford town.

Whitewashed cottage near Kinvara, Co. Galway.

Cottage at Malin Beag, Co. Donegal. The roped and pegged down thatch is a feature of the Donegal cottage, and rarely found elsewhere in Ireland.

Cottage at Bolus Head, Co. Kerry.

Home for tea. A small cottage in the village of Milltown Malbay, Co. Clare.

Cottage at the foot of Croagh Patrick mountain, Co. Mayo.

Cottage window near Wexford Town.